Pebble Plus
Bilingüe/ Bilingual

GENTE DE LAS FUERZAS ARMADAS DE EE.UU./PEOPLE OF THE U.S. ARMED FORCES

MARINES
DE LA INFANTERÍA DE MARINA DE EE.UU.

MARINES
OF THE U.S. MARINE CORPS

por/by Jennifer Reed

Editora consultora/Consulting Editor: Gail Saunders-Smith, PhD

CAPSTONE PRESS
a capstone imprint

Pebble Plus is published by Capstone Press,
151 Good Counsel Drive, P.O. Box 669, Mankato, Minnesota 56002.
www.capstonepub.com

Books published by Capstone Press are manufactured with paper
containing at least 10 percent post-consumer waste.

Library of Congress Cataloging-in-Publication Data
Reed, Jennifer, 1967–
  [Marines of the U.S. Marine Corps. Spanish & English]
  Marines de la Infantería de Marina de EE. UU. / por Jennifer Reed =
Marines of the U.S. Marine Corps / by Jennifer Reed.
  p. cm.—(Pebble Plus bilingüe. Gente de las fuerzas armadas de EE. UU. = Pebble Plus bilingual.
People of the armed forces)
  Includes index.
  Summary: "A brief introduction to a Marine's life in the Marine Corps, including training, jobs, and life after service—
in both English and Spanish"—Provided by publisher.
  ISBN 978-1-4296-6116-4 (library binding)
  1. United States. Marine Corps—Juvenile literature. I. Title. II. Title: Marines de la Infantería de Marina de Estados
Unidos. III. Title: Marines of the U.S. Marine Corps. IV. Title: Marines of the United States Marine Corps.
VE23.R43817 2011
359.9'60973—dc22   2010041503

Editorial Credits
Gillia Olson, editor; Strictly Spanish, translation services; Renée T. Doyle, designer; Danielle Ceminksy,
    bilingual book designer; Laura Manthe, production specialist

Photo Credits
AP Images/Gerry Broome, 15
Capstone Press/Karon Dubke, 21
Defense Imagery, 5; LCPL Matthew J. Anderson, USMC, 19; LCPL Nicholas J. Galvin, 7
Shutterstock/yossi, 22–23
USAF photo by SSGT Reynaldo Ramon, 17
U.S. Marine Corps photo by Cpl. Andrew J. Carlson, cover; by Cpl. Sheila M. Brooks, 9; by LCPL Marcus D Henry, 11
U.S. Navy Photo by PH3 Julianne F. Metzger, 13

Artistic Effects
iStockphoto/philpell (compass), 2–3, 24
Shutterstock/iNNOCENt (white sand), cover, 1

Note to Parents and Teachers

The Gente de las Fuerzas Armadas de EE.UU./People of the U.S. Armed Forces series
supports national science standards related to science, technology, and society. This book
describes and illustrates Marines of the U.S. Marine Corps in both English and Spanish. The
images support early readers in understanding the text. The repetition of words and phrases
helps early readers learn new words. This book also introduces early readers to subject-specific
vocabulary words, which are defined in the Glossary section. Early readers may need assistance
to read some words and to use the Table of Contents, Glossary, Internet Sites, and Index
sections of the book.

Printed in the United States of America in North Mankato, Minnesota.
092010   005933CGS11

Table of Contents

Tabla de contenidos

Joining the Marines

Men and women join the Marine Corps to protect the United States. They work on land, at sea, and in the air.

Unirse a los marines

Hombres y mujeres se unen a la Infantería de Marina para proteger a Estados Unidos. Ellos trabajan en tierra, en el mar y en el aire.

Recruits exercise and study
at basic training for 12 weeks.
The Marine Corps has
the longest basic training
in the U.S. military.

Los reclutas hacen ejercicios y

estudian en entrenamiento básico

durante 12 semanas. La Infantería

de Marina tiene el entrenamiento

básico más largo en las Fuerzas

Armadas de EE.UU.

Job Training

After basic training, recruits become
Marines. Next, they train for their jobs.
Some Marines fly helicopters, like the
CH-53E Super Stallion.

Entrenamiento para el trabajo

Después del entrenamiento básico,
los reclutas se convierten en marines.
Luego se entrenan para sus trabajos.
Algunos marines pilotean helicópteros,
como el CH-53E Super Stallion.

Many Marines are infantry.
They are trained to use
weapons and fight in battles.

Muchos marines son infantería.
Ellos son entrenados para usar
armas y pelear en batallas.

Some Marines learn
to drive tanks or AAVs.
AAVs drive on land
and float on water.

Algunos marines aprenden a
conducir tanques o AAV.
Los AAV van por tierra y
flotan en el agua.

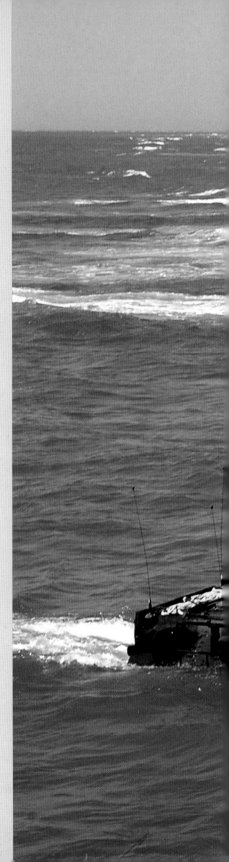

Living on Base

Marines and their families live on bases. Bases are like small towns. They have stores, hospitals, and homes.

Vivir en la base

Los marines y sus familias viven en bases. Las bases son como pequeñas ciudades. Éstas tienen tiendas, hospitales y casas.

14

The Marine Corps has 21 bases.
Bases are in the United States
and around the world.

La Infantería de Marina
tiene 21 bases. Las bases están
en Estados Unidos y alrededor
del mundo.

Serving the Country

Most Marines serve for four years. Career Marines stay in the Marine Corps for at least 20 years.

Servir al país

La mayoría de los marines sirve durante cuatro años. Los marines de carrera permanecen en la Infantería de Marina durante por lo menos 20 años.

After serving, Marines leave the Marine Corps. They are then called civilians. As civilians, they go to college or find jobs.

Después de cumplir el servicio, los marines dejan la Infantería de Marina. Entonces se los llama civiles. Como civiles, ellos van a la universidad o buscan trabajo.

Glossary

AAV—a vehicle that drives on land and floats on water; AAV stands for Assault Amphibian Vehicle

base—an area run by the military where people serving in the military live and military supplies are stored

basic training—the first training period for people who join the military

civilian—a person who is not in the military

infantry—a group of people in the military trained to fight on land

recruit—a person who has just joined the military

Internet Sites

FactHound offers a safe, fun way to find Internet sites related to this book. All of the sites on FactHound have been researched by our staff.

Here's all you do:

Visit *www.facthound.com*

Type in this code: 9781429661164

Super-cool stuff!

Check out projects, games and lots more at
www.capstonekids.com

Glosario

AAV—un vehículo que anda en tierra y flota en el agua; AAV es una sigla del inglés que significa vehículo de asalto anfibio

la base—un área administrada por las Fuerzas Armadas donde vive la gente en servicio y donde se almacenan los suministros militares

civil—una persona que no está en las Fuerzas Armadas

el entrenamiento básico—el primer período de entrenamiento para quienes se unen a la Fuerzas Armadas

la infantería—un grupo de personas en las Fuerzas Armadas entrenadas para pelear en tierra

el recluta—una persona que recién se unió a las Fuerzas Armadas

Sitios de Internet

FactHound brinda una forma segura y divertida de encontrar sitios de Internet relacionados con este libro. Todos los sitios en FactHound han sido investigados por nuestro personal.

Esto es todo lo que tienes que hacer:

Visita *www.facthound.com*

Ingresa este código: 9781429661164

¡Algo súper divertido! Hay proyectos, juegos y mucho más en www.capstonekids.com

Index

Índice